POCKET PARADIGMS

for Biblical Greek

Nicholas G. Piotrowski

CONTENTS

The Koine Greek Noun System 1

   The Definite Article

   Noun Case Endings Chart

   Lemma Endings (for Discerning Declen.)

   Prepositions

The Koine Greek Verb System 5

   Indicative εἰμί Paradigms

   Non-Indicative εἰμί Paradigms

   Indicative Person, Number, & Voice Form.

   Indicative Tense Form. without Augment

   Indicative Tense Form. with Augment

   Indicative Tense Form. with Reduplication

   Some Common Irregular Lexemes

   Some Slightly Irregular Lexemes

   Subjunctive Tense & Voice Formation

   Present & 2nd Aorist Imperative Form.

   1st Aorist Imperative Formation

   Indicative Tense Form. for -μι Verbs

Koine Greek Participles and Infinitives 17

   Present & Perfect Participle Form.

   Aorist Participle Formation

   Infinitive Tense & Voice Formation

Appendix:

A Quick-Reference Method to Parsing &
   Translating 20

   An Approach to Parsing

   An Approach to Translating

   Translating Participles

FORWARD

I began my felicitous study of biblical languages over 15 years ago. I started with Hebrew, and to this day I still use Mark Futato's *Pocket Paradigms for Biblical Hebrew* as a quick reference guide. While the goal of that work is to help students gain a mastery of the paradigms, I admit that it has a permanent place within arm's reach on my desk. It's reliable, simple and fast.

Over the past eight years I've been teaching Greek to undergraduate and graduate students, to whom I've always provided a quick-reference tool similar to Futato's for Hebrew. While there were (and still are) other condensed summaries of Greek paradigms and morphological patterns, none seemed as user-friendly as I wanted or my students needed. Some I have found were simply too big or, while reduced in size, were too cluttered.

When looking for an answer to my morphological inquiry, my eye did not know where to go, and it became difficult to explain to students. The value of this study and reference tool is found in that age-old maxim, "less is more." It is organized, therefore, to provide quick *answers to related grammatical questions on one page*. If students know which page/s to consult—the logic of which I explain below—not only will they have their answer, but also reinforce the necessary memorization as they organize the different parts of speech in their own minds.

My hope, therefore, is that this will serve as a suitable counterpart to Futato's; equally reliable, simple and fast.

HOW THIS GUIDE WORKS

The logic of this study guide is directly related to the Greek morphological system itself. With nouns, the key is to first discern the declension, and then from there identify how the "lemma" (the memorized vocabulary word/lexical form) has changed its ending. Therein lies the case and number. With finite verbs, the first question is whether there is an augment or reduplication. From there one is well on their way to discerning the tense and mood, and can then move on to person, number and voice, again in the ending. And participles combine these steps. In other words, it's all about "morphemes"—the various letters at particular locations in words that carry the inflected meaning.

Therefore, the first skill needed for using this guide is a precise vocabulary. Know the vocabulary well, including spellings, so that you can discern where the morphemes (those little changes) are. Then this study tool will help you organize and memorize the recurring morphemes. In this study guide **the specific and unique morpheme** to notice in any word **is boldfaced**. Look for them in words; find them on the appropriate page. After some time they will also sink into your long-term memory.

There is another value to learning vocabulary words (lemmas) perfectly. It is not only morphemes that help carry the inflected meaning but the "stem" as well. Typically grammars will instruct you to learn the six "principle parts"—the six slightly nuanced word stems for any given lemma. One should certainly learn principle parts when they are able, but for starting out they can be very difficult to grasp. But, if you know the lemma you do not need the principle parts because parsing a word *only necessitates knowing whether the stem has changed from its lexical form* (the "lemma") *which is always in the present tense* (for verbs). Therefore, another element of this guide is the heuristic question to ask of any verb: **"Is this word built on the present tense stem?"** That is, is the spelling of the stem the same as the memorized vocabulary word? Asking this question differentiates some aorist forms from imperfects, and so forth.

In the end you are looking for morphemes, and occasionally asking if the stem spelling has changed from the lexical form/lemma/vocabulary word. Both require a good grasp of Greek vocabulary. From there, this guide will help you identify the morphemes and altered spellings on your way to precise parsing and translation.

LESS COMMON ABBREVIATIONS

m/p	middle or passive
aug.	augment
redup.	reduplication
pr.t.s.?	Is this word built on the <u>pr</u>esent <u>t</u>ense <u>s</u>tem? (Is this word's stem spelled the same as the lemma?)
t. form.	tense formative
m. form.	mood formative
conn. v.	connecting vowel

The Definite Article

	2	1	2
	masc	fem	neut
nom sg	ὁ	ἡ	τό
gen sg	τοῦ	τῆς	τοῦ
dat sg	τῷ	τῇ	τῷ
acc sg	τόν	τήν	τό
nom pl	οἱ	αἱ	τά
gen pl	τῶν	τῶν	τῶν
dat pl	τοῖς	ταῖς	τοῖς
acc pl	τούς	τάς	τά

Noun Case Endings Chart

	2	1	2	3	3
	masc	fem	neut	masc/fem	neut
nom sg	ος	α/η	ον	ς	-
gen sg	ου	ας/ης	ου	ος	ος
dat sg	ῳ	ᾳ/ῃ	ῳ	ι	ι
acc sg	ον	αν/ην	ον	α/ν	-
nom pl	οι	αι	α	ες	α
gen pl	ων	ων	ων	ων	ων
dat pl	οις	αις	οις	σι(ν)	σι(ν)
acc pl	ους	ας	α	ας	α

Most common vocative endings: -ε, -οι, -ες, or no ending.

Lemma Endings
(for Discerning Declension)

2ⁿᵈ decl: 1ˢᵗ decl: 3ʳᵈ decl:

-ος   -η   -μα (-μα∓)

-ον   -α   -ις

-Most endings not in the box are 3ʳᵈ declension!

3

Prepositions

Lex. f.:	Alt. spellings:		w/ genitive:	w/dative:	w/ accusative:
ἀνα	ἀν᾽				among/between/upwards
ἀντί			instead/in place of		
διά	δι᾽		through		on account of/for the
ἐκ		ἐξ	from/out of		sake of/because
ἔξω			outside (as adverb: without)		
ἀπό	ἀπ᾽	ἀφ᾽	away from		
κατά	κατ᾽	καθ᾽	down from/against		according to/during
μετά	μετ᾽	μεθ᾽	with		after/behind
σύν				with/in association	
ἐπί	ἐπ᾽	ἐφ᾽	on/over/when	on the basis of/at	on/to/against
περί	περ᾽		about/concerning		around
παρά	παρ᾽		from	beside/in presence	alongside of
ἐνώπιον			before		
πρό			before/in front of		
πρός					to/toward/with
ὑπέρ			on behalf of/concerning/in place of		above/over
ὑπό	ὑπ᾽	ὑφ᾽	by		under
εἰς					into/in/among
ἐν				in/on/among	
χωρίς			without/apart from/separately		

Indicative εἰμί Paradigms

<u>Present</u> tense:

1st sing	εἰμί	I am
2nd sing	εἶ	you are
3rd sing	ἐστίν/ἐστί	he/she/it is
1st pl	ἐσμέν	we are
2nd pl	ἐστέ	you all are
3rd pl	εἰσίν/εἰσί	they are

[note the circumflex!]

<u>Future</u> tense [note paradigm takes middle forms]:

1st sing	ἔσομαι	I will be
2nd sing	ἔσῃ	you will be
3rd sing	ἔσται	he/she/it will be
1st pl	ἐσόμεθα	we will be
2nd pl	ἔσεσθε	you all will be
3rd pl	ἔσονται	they will be

<u>Imperfect</u> tense [note lexemes have an augment and 2° endings]:

1st sing	ἤμην	I was
2nd sing	ἦς/ἦσθα	you were
3rd sing	ἦν	he/she/it was
1st pl	ἦμεν/ἤμεθα	we were
2nd pl	ἦτε	you all were
3rd pl	ἦσαν	they were

Verbs

5

Non-Indicative εἰμί Paradigms

<u>Present Active Subjunctive</u>:

1st sing	ὦ	I would be
2nd sing	ᾖς	you would be
3rd sing	ᾖ	he/she/it would be
1st pl	ὦμεν	we would be
2nd pl	ἦτε	you all would be
3rd pl	ὦσι(ν)	they would be

<u>Present Active Imperative</u>:

2nd sing	ἴσθι	be!
3rd sing	ἔστω	he/she/it/ must be!
2nd pl	ἔστε	be!
3rd pl	ἔστωσαν	they must be!

<u>Present Active Infinitive</u>:

Active	εἶναι	to be

<u>Present Active Participle</u>:

	3	1	3		3	1	3	
	masc	fem	neut		masc	fem	neut	
nom sg	ὤν	οὖσα	ὄν	nom pl	ὄντες	οὖσαι	ὄντα	being
gen sg	ὄντος	οὔσης	ὄντος	gen pl	ὄντων	οὐσῶν	ὄντων	
dat sg	ὄντι	οὔσῃ	ὄντι	dat pl	οὖσι(ν)	οὔσαις	οὖσι(ν)	
acc sg	ὄντα	οὖσαν	ὄν	acc pl	ὄντας	οὔσας	ὄντα	

<u>Present Active Optative</u>:

3rd sing	εἴη	it could be

Indicative Person, #, & Voice Formation

	w/o aug.:	w/ aug.:	w/ redup.:	pres. μι:
1 sg act*	λύω	ἔλυον (1st aor: ἔλυσα)	-α	-μι
2 sg act	λύεις	ἔλυες	-ας	-ς
3 sg act	λύει	ἔλυε(ν)	-ε(ν)	-σι(ν)
1 pl act	λύομεν	ἐλύομεν	-αμεν	-μεν
2 pl act	λύετε	ἐλύετε	-ατε	-τε
3 pl act	λύουσι(ν)	ἔλυον (aor pass: -σαν)	-ασι(ν) or -αν	-ασι(ν)
1 sg m/p	λύομαι	ἐλυόμην	-μαι	-μαι
2 sg m/p	λύῃ (σαι)	ἐλύου (σο) (1st aor: -σω)	-σαι	-σαι
3 sg m/p	λύεται	ἐλύετο	-ται	-ται
1 pl m/p	λυόμεθα	ἐλυόμεθα	-μεθα	-μεθα
2 pl m/p	λύεσθε	ἐλύεσθε	-σθε	-σθε
3 pl m/p	λύονται	ἐλύοντο	-νται	-νται

* Aorist passives take active suffixes.

Indicative Tense Formation
<u>without</u> Augment

	aug.	pr.t.s.?	t. form.	1st sing. example	infl. meaning
pres act		yes		λύω	I am loosing
pres m/p		yes		λύομαι	I am being loosed
pres dep		yes		πορεύομαι	I am going
fut act		some	σ	λύσω	I will loose
fut mid		some	σ	λύσομαι	I will loose myself
fut dep		some	σ	πορεύσομαι	I will go
liq fut act		rare	λˆ/μˆ/νˆ/ρˆ[1]	μενῶ	I will remain
liq fut mid		rare	λˆ/μˆ/νˆ/ρˆ[1]	μενοῦμαι	I will remain
1st fut pas		often	θησ	λυθήσομαι	I will be loosed
2nd fut pas		some	ησ	ἀποσταλήσομαι	I will be sent

[1]The real tense formative is εσ, but when the σ drops out (εϴ) the lexemes look like this:
λοῦ/λεῖ/λῶ/λῇ/μοῦ/μεῖ/μῶ/μῇ/νοῦ/νεῖ/νῶ/νῇ/ροῦ/ρεῖ/ρῶ/ρῇ.

Indicative Tense Formation
<u>with</u> Augment

	aug.	pr.t.s.?	t. form.	1st sing. example	infl. meaning
imp act	ε	yes		ἔλυον	I was loosing
imp m/p	ε	yes		ἐλυόμην	I was being loosed
imp dep	ε	yes		ἐπορευόμην	I was going
1st aor act	ε	often	σα	ἔλυσα	I loosed
1st aor mid	ε	often	σα	ἐλυσάμην	I loosed myself
1st aor dep	ε	often	σα	ἐπορεύσαμην	I went
liq aor act	ε	rare	λα/μα/να/ρα[1]	ἔμεινα	I remained
2nd aor act	ε	**no**		ἔλαβον	I took
2nd aor m/d	ε	**no**		ἐγενόμην	I became
1st aor pas	ε	often	(σ)θη	ἐλύθην[2]	I was loosed
2nd aor pas	ε	some	η	ἐγράφην[2]	I was written

[1]The real tense formative is σα, but when the σ drops out (ᶿα). [2]Aorist passive takes active suffixes.

Indicative Tense Formation
with <u>Reduplication</u>

	<u>redup.</u>	<u>pr.t.s.?</u>	<u>t. form.</u>	<u>1st sing. example</u>	<u>infl. Meaning</u>
1st pft act	(λε)	some	κα	λέλυκα	I have loosed
2nd pft act	(γε)	some	α	γέγονα	I have become
pft m/p	(λε)	some		λέλυμαι[1]	I have been loosed
pft dep	(πε)	some		πεπόρευμαι[1]	I have gone

[1]Note the lack of connecting vowel.

Some Common Irregular Lexemes

εἶχον — I was having (imp of ἔχω)

ἔξω — I will have (fut of ἔχω; ≠ ἔξω)

ἔσχον — I had (aor of ἔχω)

ἐλεύσομαι — I will go (fut dep of ἔρχομαι)

ἦλθον — I went (aor of ἔρχομαι)

ἐλήλυθα — I have gone (perf of ἔρχομαι)

ἐρῶ — I will say (fut of λέγω)

εἶπον — I said (aor of λέγω; alt: εἶπαν)

ὄψομαι — I will see (fut dep of ὁράω/βλέπω)

εἶδον — I saw (aor of ὁράω/βλέπω)

πεσοῦμαι — I will fall (fut dep of πίπτω)

γνώσομαι — I will know (fut dep of γινώσκω)

ἔγνων — I knew (aor of γινώσκω)

χαρήσομαι — I will rejoice (fut dep of χαίρω)

λήμψομαι — I will take (fut dep of λαμβάνω)

εἴληφα — I have taken (perf of λαμβάνω)

ἀκήκοα — I have heard (perf of ἀκούω)

φάγομαι — I will eat (fut dep of ἐσθίω)

ἔφαγον — I ate (aor of ἐσθίω)

ἔφη — he said (aor/imp of φημί)

οἴσω — I will carry (fut of φέρω)

ἤνεγκα — I carried (aor of φέρω)

ἰδών — upon seeing (aor ptc of ὁράω)

ἐλθών — upon coming (aor ptc of ἔρχομαι)

εἰπών — upon saying (aor ptc of λέγω)

εἰδώς — having known (perf ptc of οἶδα)

εἰπέ — say!/tell! (aor imper of λέγω)

ἐλθέ — go!/come! (aor imper of ἔρχομαι)

Some *Slightly* Irregular Lexemes

βήσομαι — I will go (fut dep of βαίνω)

γενήσομαι — I will become (fut dep of γίνομαι)

γέγονα — I have become (perf of γίνομαι)

ἑώρακα — I have seen (perf of ὁράω/βλέπω)

ὤφθην — I was seen (aor pass of ὁράω/βλέπω)

ἐπορεύθην — I went (aor pass *form* of πορεύομαι)

ἔπεσον — I fell (aor of πίπτω)

ῥηθείς — upon being said (aor pass ptc of λέγω)

ἐρρέθην — I was said (aor pass of λέγω)

ἐνεγκών — upon carrying (aor ptc of φέρω)

ἤχθην — I was led (aor pass of ἄγω)

ἤγαγον — I led (aor of ἄγω)

ἐβλήθην — I was thrown (aor pass of βάλλω)

κηρύξω — I will proclaim (fut act of κηρύσσω)

ἐκήρυξω — I proclaimed (aor act of κηρύσσω)

Subjunctive Tense & Voice Formation

	pr.t.s.?	t. form.+m. form.	1st sing. example	infl. meaning
pres act	yes*	ω/η¹	λύω	I would be loosing
pres m/p/d	yes	ω/η¹	λύωμαι	I would be loosed
1st aor act	often	σω/ση¹	λύσω²	I would loose
1st aor mid	often	σω/ση¹	λύσωμαι	I would loose myself
2nd aor act	**no**	ω/η¹	λάβω	I would take
2nd aor m/d	**no**	ω/η¹	γένωμαι	I would become
1st aor pas	often	θῶ/θῇ	λυθῶ³	I would be loosed
2nd aor pas	some	ῶ/ῇ¹	γραφῶ³	I would be written

*Indicative and Subjunctive contract verbs almost always look identical.
¹Pay attention to 1st singular actives (λύω/λύσω); the lengthened connecting vowel causes them to look like indicatives. Also, the 3rd singular actives and 2nd singular middles (λύῃ/λύσῃ) look like 2nd singular middle indicatives. And look our for liquids in the 1st aorist active and middle.
²Note the lack of an augment. ³Aorist passive takes active suffixes.

13

Present & 2nd Aorist Imperative Formation

	pr.t.s.?	conn. v.	m. form.	1st sing. ex.	infl. meaning
pres act 2 sg	yes	ϵ^2		λῦε[1]	be loosing!
pres act 3 sg	yes	ϵ	τω	λυέτω	he must be loosing!
pres act 2 pl	yes	ϵ	τε	λύετε	be loosing!
pres act 3 pl	yes	ϵ	τωσαν	λυέτωσαν	they must be loosing!
pres m/p 2 sg	yes	ου[3]		λύου	be being loosed!
pres m/p 3 sg	yes	ϵ	σθω	λυέσθω	he must be being loosed!
pres m/p 2 pl	yes	ϵ	σθε	λύεσθε	be being loosed!
pres m/p 3 pl	yes	ϵ	σθωσαν	λυέσθωσαν	they must be being loosed!
2nd aor act -	**no**	ϵ^4	τω/τε/τωσαν	λάβε	take!
2nd aor m/d -	**no**	ου[5]/ϵ	σθω/σθε/σθωσαν	γενοῦ	become!
2nd aor pass -	some	η*	τι/τω/τε/τωσαν	γράφητι	be written!

[1]The 2nd per. sing. pres. act. endings for contract verbs are: α, ει, and ου (ἀγάπα, ποίει, and πλήρου).
[2]μι verbs: η, ει, ου, or υ. [3]μι verbs: σο. [4]μι verbs: θι, ος, or ες. [5]Or ω for μι verbs. *Actually a tense formative.

1st Aorist Imperative Formation

	pr.t.s.?	t. form.	m. form.	1st sing. ex.	infl. meaning
1st aor act 2 sg	often	σ	ον	λῦσον	loose!
1st aor act 3 sg	often	σα	τω	λυσάτω	he must loose!
1st aor act 2 pl	often	σα	τε	λύσατε	loose!
1st aor act 3 pl	often	σα	τωσαν	λυσάτωσαν	they must loose!
1st aor mid 2 sg	often	σ	αι	λῦσαι¹	loose yourself!
1st aor mid 3 sg	often	σα	σθω	λυσάσθω	he must loose himself!
1st aor mid 2 pl	often	σα	σθε	λύσασθε	loose yourselves!
1st aor mid 3 pl	often	σα	σθωσαν	λυσάσθωσαν	they must loose th'selves!
1st aor pas 2 sg	often	θη	τι	λύθητι	be loosed!
1st aor pas 3 sg	often	θη	τω	λυθήτω	he must be loosed!
1st aor pas 2 pl	often	θη	τε	λύθητε	be loosed!
1st aor pas 3 pl	often	θη	τωσαν	λυθήτωσαν	they must be loosed!

¹Looks like 1st aorist active infinitive.

Indicative Tense Formation of -μι Verbs

	aug.	redup.	t. form.	1st sing. example	infl. meaning
pres act/mid/pas		(δι)		δίδωμι[1]	I am giving
imp act/mid/pas	ε	(δι)		ἐδίδουν[2]	I was giving
fut act/mid			σ	δώσω	I will give
fut pas			θησ	δοθήσομαι	I will be given
aor act/mid	ε		κα	**ἔδωκα**	I gave
aor pas	ε		θη	ἐδόθην[3]	I was given
perf act		(δε)	κα	δέδωκα	I have given
perf mid/pas		(δε)		δέδομαι	I have been given

[1]Notice that the stem vowel sometimes lengthens and sometimes does not (the root of δίδωμι is δο), and in some words drops out. [2]The 3rd sing. imp. act. ind. is ἐδίδου. [3]Aorist passives take active suffixes.

Present & Perfect Participle Formation

			redup.	t. form.	decl.	nom. sg. ex.	infl. meaning
pres	act	m/n		οντ	3	λύ<u>ων</u>[1]	while loosing
pres	act	f		ουσα	1	λύουσα	while loosing
pres	m/p/d	m/n		ομενο	2	λυόμενος	while being loosed
pres	m/p/d	f		ομενη	1	λυομένη	while being loosed
perf	act	m/n	(λε)	κοτ	3	λελυ**κώς**	having loosed
perf	act	f	(λε)	κυια	1	λελυκυῖα	having loosed
perf	m/p/d	m/n	(λε)	μενο*	2	λελυμένος	having been loosed
perf	m/p/d	f	(λε)	μενη*	1	λελυμένη	having been loosed

Participles & Infinites

[1]Nom. masc. sing. pres. act. ptc. endings for μι verbs: ας, εις, ους, υς. *Note the lack of connecting vowel.

Aorist Participle Formation

	pr.t.s.?	t. form.	decl.	nom. sg. ex.	infl. meaning
1st aor act m/n	often	σαντ[1]	3	λύσας	upon loosing
1st aor act f	often	σασα[1]	1	λύσασα	upon loosing
1st aor m/d m/n	often	σαμενο[1]	2	λυσάμενος	upon loosing for himself
1st aor m/d f	often	σαμενη[1]	1	λυσαμένη	upon loosing for herself
1st aor pas m/n	often	θεντ	3	λυθείς	upon being loosed
1st aor pas f	often	θεισα	1	λυθεῖσα	upon being loosed
2nd aor act m/n	no	οντ[3]	3	βαλών[2]	upon throwing
2nd aor act f	no	ουσα[3]	1	βαλοῦσα	upon throwing
2nd aor m/d m/n	no	ομενο[3]	2	γενόμενος	upon becoming
2nd aor m/d f	no	ομενη[3]	1	γενομένη	upon becoming
2nd aor pas m/n	some	εντ	3	γραφείς	upon being written
2nd aor pas f	some	εισα	1	γραφεῖσα	upon being written

[1]Look out for liquids. [2]Nom. masc. sing. 2nd aor. act. ptc. endings for μι verbs: ας, εις, ους, υς.
[3]The different stem is the only way to distinguish the 2nd aor ptc from the pres ptc.

Infinitive Tense & Voice Formation

	redup.	pr.t.s.?	t. form.+m. form.[1]	1st sing.	infl. meaning
pres act[2]		yes	$\epsilon\iota\nu$[3]$/\nu\alpha\iota$	λύειν	to be loosing
pres m/p/d		yes	$\epsilon\sigma\theta\alpha\iota$	λύεσθαι	to be loosed
1st aor act		often	$\sigma\alpha\iota$*	λύσαι	to loose
1st aor mid		often	$\sigma\alpha\sigma\theta\alpha\iota$*	λύσασθαι	to loose myself
2nd aor act		**no**	$\epsilon\iota\nu/\nu\alpha\iota$	λαβεῖν	to take
2nd aor m/d		**no**	$\epsilon\sigma\theta\alpha\iota$	γενέσθαι	to become
1st aor pas		often	$\theta\eta\nu\alpha\iota$	λυθῆναι	to be loosed
2nd aor pas		some	$\eta\nu\alpha\iota$	γραφῆναι	to be written
perf act	(λε)	some	$\kappa\epsilon\nu\alpha\iota$	λελυκέναι	to have loosed
perf m/p/d	(λε)	some	$\sigma\theta\alpha\iota$	λελύσθαι	to have been loosed

[1]Infinitives do not carry person or number. [2] The present active infinitive of εἰμί is εἶναι (to be).
[3]On contract verbs ending in α, and in o, the present active infinitive endings are ᾶν/ῆν and οῦν respectively.
*Look out for liquids.

19

An Approach to Parsing

- Find the lemma.   ἐγν<u>ώσ</u>θης from γινώσκω
- Divide verbs & ptcs. into 4 parts.   ἐ/γνώσ/θη/ς
  - Augment or Reduplication   ἐ
  - Stem*   γνώσ
  - Tense and/or Mood formative   θη
  - Noun or Verb Ending   ς
- Divide nouns into two parts.   θρόν/οις
  - Stem   θρόν
  - Case formative   οις

*This is where the stem "changes" occur in 2nd aorists (ἔγνωτε).

An Approach to Translating

- Divide sentence into clauses.
- Find the verb(s) in each clause.[1]
  - Is it a present verb?
  - Does it have an augment and/or a 2° ending?
    - If so what's the tense formative? Has the stem changed?
  - Does it have a reduplication?
- Find the nominative noun(s) in each clause.[2]
- Translate the rest of the clause, noting agreement.
  - Rest of clause revolves around nom. noun and finite verb.
- Put it all together in a transl. that reflects the Greek.

[1]If a clause doesn't have a verb you may need to supply a "to be" verb.
[2]In some clauses the subject is part of the verb and there is no nominative noun.

Translating Participles

- First find lemma and divide word into parts.
- Next, find the case, number, and gender.
  - This is, of course, in the case ending.
- Third, find the tense.
  - Look for the tense formative, or the changed stem.
- Fourth, find the voice.
  - This is also in the tense formative.
- Fifth, discern if it's adv. or adj., attr. or subst.
  - Is it articular or not? What noun(s) does it agree with?
- Finally, put the participle together with the noun or pronoun it agrees with and relate it to the main verb.

Πᾶς οὖν ὅστις ἀκούει μου τοὺς λόγους τούτους καὶ ποιεῖ αὐτούς, ὁμοιωθήσεται ἀνδρὶ φρονίμῳ, ὅστις ᾠκοδόμησεν αὐτοῦ τὴν οἰκίαν ἐπὶ τὴν πέτραν.